Conversations of Tao

Mark Tarver

http://www.fast-print.net/bookshop

CONVERSATIONS OF TAOIST MASTER FU HSIANG
Copyright © Dr Mark Tarver 2015

ISBN 978-178456-233-5

First published 2015 by Inner Spirit Press,
An imprint of Fast-Print Publishing of
Peterborough, England.

Contents

Dedication

This book is written in loving dedication to Magdalena Pamesa M.D. (1940-2010), friend, healer and ally, who fought with me against an ancient evil. May her spirit find rest.

Introduction

Some of the elements of these dialogues originate from a course on Taoist philosophy and exercise which I taught as part of a course in internal alchemy in 2001. Every session was divided into a physical, emotional and a philosophical component. My students were led to practice Taoist yoga and experiment with Taoist meditation techniques. They also used powerful visualisation and releasing techniques to explore their own emotions. The philosophical part of the course, was aimed to develop their awareness of the nature of evil, since evil in one form or another, affects everybody on this planet. What I was aiming to do was to restore the balance that should exist in all human beings, by simultaneously exercising their bodies, their emotions and their intellects.

The course taught me a lot. It saved the life of one person who would otherwise have killed herself and it taught me about the destructive nature of the trapped emotions that people harbour. These emotions made it impossible for me to continue the experiment. However, after the group was disbanded, the philosophical component of the course stayed in my mind. I wrote an illustrated essay on the course, trying to convey some of the philosophy of the course. But the essay was partial and unfinished, so I laid it aside for three years to concentrate on science.

In 2004, I felt the impulse to try to finish it. A friend phoned me and told me that an acquaintance of hers had decided to write a dialogue on Buddhism and this gave me the thought that a dialogue was the natural vehicle to express these ideas.

The result is this series of short dialogues organised around a Taoist class, composed of a master and two students. The setting of the dialogue is thus not too dissimilar from the setting in which these ideas were created. The class is smaller than my own, since the demands of dialogue require a small number of people. Here there are three, the master Fu Hsiang and the students Li Chen and Zhi Peng.

Initially, my first thought was to set these dialogues in some remote part of Chinese history. But this would be inconvenient, since many insights about human nature and the natural world were not available to the ancients. Rather than maroon the discussion in first century science, I placed it to the present day. So there are references to current events and facts about natural history and chemistry which are products of Western science.

Another reason for avoiding the ancient past, is that authenticity requires that the speech and outlook of the characters in these dialogues would conform to what existed in China two millennia ago. But without detailed historical research (and even with detailed historical research) it is extremely difficult to reconstruct the mindset of the ancient Chinese. Nothing is more ludicrous than a filmmaker who attempts to reconstruct the past of another country and succeeds only in producing characters who dress in ruffles and act like Manhattan stockbrokers.

Accordingly, the Taoist master Fu Hsiang is a master for the modern times. He is comfortable with the past and the future, and his knowledge of Taoist practice and modern science places him squarely in the twenty-first century. The archaic manner of address which his students use, always addressing him as *sifu* or *master*, is in accordance with ancient tradition which accords the teacher in China a status which he has lost in the West.

Amongst Western philosophers, Plato is best known for having conducted his philosophical expositions in the form of dialogues.   His early dialogues are almost dramatic compositions in their own right and could be performed as plays.   The later dialogues, including the *Republic*, are more stilted and show the effect of the message overcoming the medium.   The central character is always Socrates; but whilst in the early dialogues, there is an interplay between the characters, in the later dialogues Socrates dominates to the point where the other characters are almost reduced to yes-men.

Steering a dialogue between the two extremes of a free-for-all, where no message is communicated, and one where all characters are subordinated to the message, requires some care.   Accordingly, the structure of the dialogues reflects the natural progression of an argument, with Li Chen and Zhi Peng sometimes challenging Fu Hsiang over what they believe are contradictions.   Their characters are different; Li Chen is a devout Buddhist, kind-hearted and a family person. Zhi Peng is college-educated, sharper, more questioning and more worldly than Li Chen.

Fu Hsiang, for his part, is not unlike Socrates, in that his questions are designed to lead the students to knowledge by exposing the contradictions in their thinking.   His technique, of asking apparently irrelevant questions and then accumulating the answers into a refutation of his student's position or a defence of his own, are very much in the spirit of the *elenchus* of Socrates. It is my hope that these dialogues will be read by people who are interested in the spirit and practice of Taoism.

嬰兒現形圖

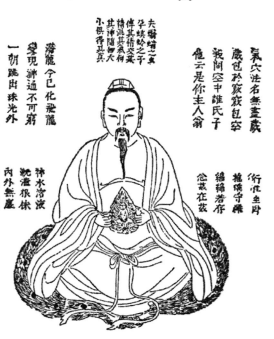

此時丹熟更須憂嬰兒

氣穴法名無盡藏
歲包於寂寂包空
我問空中誰氏子
他云是你主人翁

衍住坐卧
拖擺守雅
綿綿若存
念兹在兹

夫嬰緒之東
華填鈴之子
俾其情交媾
情況其系利
其神隨細大
小俱得其真

潛龍今已化飛龍
毫現神通不可窮
一朝跳出珠光外
渾身直到紫微宮

神水溶液
沈滬根株
內外無塵
長養聖躬

他日雲飛方見真人朝上帝

1

The First Discourse

The Unreality of Good and Evil

Main Characters

Li Chen ... An inner door[1] disciple of the master Fu Hsiang.

Zhi Peng ... Another inner door disciple.

Fu Hsiang ... Taoist master and adept of the Internal Arts.

Scene: *the home of Fu Hsiang. Li Chen and Zhi Peng have completed their lesson in bagua[2] from Fu Hsiang. They are resting and drinking jasmine tea in the living room of Fu Hsiang. The room is modern, but contains artifacts from ancient China, pottery adorns the furniture, and scrolls and a tai chi[3] sword hang from the wall. Li Chen is sitting in an armchair opposite Fu Hsiang and a low table lies between the two. On a third side of the table is an old settee in which Zhi Peng is lounging. The atmosphere is relaxed and friendly. The conversation is about friends.*

Li Chen: So after Guagua received the money off his father; he went straight away to spend it on the car of his dreams.   Unfortunately, 90,000 *yuan* was not enough to buy a dream car from America.   His heart was set on an SUV.   So he went to a second-hand dealer instead, who took him to a back lot and showed him such a car. It was exactly what he wanted, and he paid over 80,000 *yuan* to get it. But he had the car for only a week when it started to give him trouble. After only a month it would not start at all, and when he tried to find the man who sold it to him, he found that the lot was empty and the address he got from him was fake. So now he has an SUV that doesn't drive and the remains of his money is not enough to fix it.

Zhi Peng: Guagua is a fool whose eyes are bigger than his pockets. He should have settled for a smaller car and gone to a reputable dealer.

Li Chen: But it is not altogether his fault, the car looked good and the dealer was very persuasive. You could understand that he was hooked.

Zhi Peng: But all the same he should have had it checked. Now he is out of pocket and he has lost face as well. What do you say master?

Fu Hsiang: Guagua did not act wisely, it is true, but he has learnt a lesson. Perhaps it was worth 80,000 *yuan* to learn it. Who can say?

Li Chen: But nevertheless, we should extend our compassion to him for having fallen victim to fraud. Even if he was duped, we should not look down upon a friend who has suffered a misfortune.

Fu Hsiang: It is true that we should extend our compassion to him. But are you so sure that what befell him was evil? Can you be so certain of saying that what befalls us is good or evil?

Li Chen: Of course, for the Buddha tells us that we should follow the course of right action and right thought. This is part of the Buddhist eightfold path[4] which we are taught as part of the *dharma*[5]. We avoid doing evil and try to do good.

Fu Hsiang: So, like the Christians, you believe that good and evil are part of the external world; and not figments of the mind or inventions of society, but real and existing properties of things that happen in reality?

Li Chen: Well, yes. That is precisely what I mean.

4

Fu Hsiang: Well then, if a thing has a property, does it matter how we describe it? Doesn't it retain that property irrespective of how it is described? [6]

Li Chen: I am not sure what you mean, *sifu*[7].

Fu Hsiang: Let me give you an example. You have travelled before to the site of Chairman Mao's tomb?

Li Chen: Yes, it is by Tiananmen Square in Beijing.

Fu Hsiang: Good. And what is the largest square in Beijing?

Li Chen: Well, it is Tiananmen Square itself.

Fu Hsiang: So we could also say that Chairman Mao's tomb is by Tiananmen Square and also that Chairman Mao's tomb is by the largest square in Beijing. These are both objective facts. Wouldn't you agree?

Li Chen: Yes I would. This is obvious, I do not understand the point of your example.

Fu Hsiang: Well, what I asked you was that if a thing has a property, then does it matter how we describe that thing. For instance if the location of Mao's tomb is Tiananmen Square, we can say "Tiananmen Square is the location of Mao's tomb" or we could also say "The largest square in Beijing is the location of Mao's tomb". The point is that being the location of Mao's tomb is an objective property of Tiananmen, so it does not matter how we describe the square itself.

Li Chen: This seems clear enough.

Fu Hsiang: Well now, can you not now answer my question? If a thing has a property, then does it matter how we describe that thing?

Li Chen: It seems clear, *sifu*, that the answer you expect is 'no'. Nor can I think of any reason to give any other answer.

Fu Hsiang: This would seem the reasonable answer. If something is really a property of some object, then it does not matter how we locate the object or what description we use. For instance, who is the best Wu[8] teacher in Shanghai?

Li Chen: That would be old master Ma, who is now over eighty years old.

Fu Hsiang: So we can say both "Old master Ma is now over eighty years old" and also that "The best Wu teacher in Shanghai is over eighty years old"; since old master Ma and the best Wu teacher in Shanghai are one and the same.

Li Chen: Of course.

Fu Hsiang: When something really is a property of an object, it does not matter how we describe that object; but it retains that property no matter how we view it. Is this not your conclusion?

Li Chen: Yes.

Fu Hsiang: So now, do you still consider good and evil to be properties of events in the real world? Can you accept they are illusory?

Li Chen: It may be that I should not believe this, but I cannot see why I should not.

Zhi Peng: The history of the world is full of sad events, *sifu*. Look at the history of China, the Japanese war, the Cultural Revolution. People do not talk of these things, it is not our way. The modern way is to keep your head down and make money. We don't want to remember the past; if you lie down with ghosts, you will become a ghost. You have to accept the bad, and press on with your life.

Li Chen: That's right. My father used to speak of the barbarity of the soldiers when they came to Tibet.[9] He left Tibet and married my mother and took a Chinese name. But he often spoke about how the Chinese soldiers murdered and drove out the monks and nuns of the Buddhist orders. How can you doubt that evil is alive and existing in this world?

Fu Hsiang: These events are close to you and to all of us. It is hard to view them without attachment. But if we are to penetrate the nature of evil we must try to do so.

Li Chen: Who can contemplate these things without feeling moved in some way? It is only human.

Fu Hsiang: It is not human nature to remain unmoved where we think our interests are at stake. We need to look at events far removed from us, in order to see clearly the nature of things. Li Chen, you were talking about a book you read last week about an ancient catastrophe.

Li Chen: Ah, you mean that book about the dinosaur extinction of 65 million years ago! A meteorite came and struck the earth causing an explosion.

Fu Hsiang: And the explosion itself was significant?

Li Chen: Massive, *sifu*. The seas rose to the height of several *li*[10], and nearly ninety percent of all animal life was extinguished in one stroke. The Western scientists have shown that the effects of this shock were felt all over the world.

Fu Hsiang: A disaster then?

Li Chen: The biggest.

Fu Hsiang: Well since disasters are not good, we can say that the event that destroyed nearly all life 65 million years ago was evil.

Li Chen: I suppose you could say that.

Zhi Peng: Especially from the point of view of the dinosaurs.

Fu Hsiang: But this same event, as you told us, allowed the mammals to evolve and hence for the human race to emerge.

Li Chen: Yes; that is how it worked out.

Fu Hsiang: So we have two descriptions of the same event. We can describe it as "the event that wiped out ninety percent of animal life 65 million years ago" or as "the event that happened 65 million years ago that was the foundation for human existence". Now the first you say is a disaster, and evil, and the second you must suppose is good, if you value anything about anybody.

Li Chen: I suppose so; but this seems peculiar.

Fu Hsiang: It is certainly strange, for we are talking about the very same thing in both cases. Also we agreed that if something was a property of something then it remained so however we described it. But here we have a property that seems to appear and disappear depending on how we choose to describe the same event. But we agreed that if something really was a property of a thing, then no matter how that thing was described, it retained that property.

Li Chen: Are you are saying that good and evil are not properties of things at all?

Fu Hsiang: So it would appear. You were lamenting the events that took place in Tibet over fifty years ago. Two years ago did you not visit England to stay in a monastery?

Li Chen: I did. I once stayed with the New Kadampa Tradition in a monastery in England. My friend Gordon had invited me. They were very kind.

Fu Hsiang: I know that order. They were founded by Geshe Kelsang who is a Tibetan Buddhist - one of the exiles from that very country from where your own father came. The Tibetan Buddhists were driven from the mountains to take refuge in the West. They have flourished because of their discipline. Now the Tibetan Buddhists have more followers throughout the world then they ever had before the Chinese came. You see the paradoxical nature of evil – the invasion and butchery of 1950 was also the event that provided the greatest revival they have ever had.

Li Chen: So you are saying Guagua's misfortune was not a misfortune after all?

Fu Hsiang: Fortune and misfortune, good and evil depend on how we view events. They do not exist as properties in the same way that ordinary people regard them. The tendency for us to think this way is the foundation for much of our struggle and illusion on this physical plane.

Zhi Peng: Well I for one will count it as the greatest misfortune if I miss my dinner and that is one thing in the universe upon which we can all agree.

Fu Hsiang: You can separate a man from his shadow more easily than Zhi from his appetite. We shall pick up this discussion after our next lesson.

The Second Discourse

The Origins of the Illusion

Li Chen: *Sifu*, I have thought over our last conversation. I confess to being troubled. It seems immoral to deny the existence of evil when so obviously it seems to be all around us. For example, suppose I just hit a child at random, going down the street, wouldn't that be evil?

Fu Hsiang: As you've described it, it certainly would.

Zhi Peng: Now isn't that a contradiction? Didn't you say in the last lesson that evil does not exist?

Fu Hsiang: Not quite, perhaps, as you mean it. But no, there is no contradiction in what I have just said.

Li Chen: So *sifu*, please explain. You said that if I were to hit a child on the street for nothing then it would be evil. But you said last time that evil is an illusion. Leastways that is what I remember you saying.

Fu Hsiang: What I mean to say is that you told me a story, and in stories, good and evil do exist. This is one of the three reasons why we believe in the existence of evil.

Li Chen: So stories are important in some way to our believing in good and evil?

Fu Hsiang: Very important. You see, we are constantly making up stories as we go through life. When we are children, we read and make up fairy stories. As we grow older, we make up stories about how people think and how the universe works. Right to the end of our days, we are constantly making up stories and revising old ones. This is part of the mind's chatter – it never stops unless we learn meditation. Even in sleep the mind makes up stories and we call them dreams.

Li Chen: Master, please explain to me how stories make us believe in the existence of good and evil.

Fu Hsiang: Stories are not reality. Even true stories are not reality. Your story is not a reality. There is no such child because it is not in your nature to do such a deed, Li Chen. And if it were, and it was a real child, then it would not be a story anymore.

Zhi Peng: Is that important?

Fu Hsiang: Very important. You see a real child is a real character; a real three-dimensional being. He has a past, he has real parents, he has friends and enemies. His boundaries radiate outward indefinitely and his actions ripple outwards into the distant future and proceed from the distant past. A real person is as mysterious as the Tao. It is only our boredom and our limited perspective that cuts us off from this recognition and leads us to say "Oh, there is old Li" or old Hua or whatever. Real people are mysterious beings. Fictional people are not, and in a fictional world good and evil do exist.

Li Chen: I still don't understand.

Fu Hsiang: Let me put it this way. If you struck a real child, your action would be woven into the unfolding of the Tao. It would be more than just Li Chen hitting a child. It would be an event with more sides than a cut diamond and just as many descriptions. If you could grasp it in its entirety, you would not be able to judge it as good or evil. But when you tell a story, it has only one side. This is the side that you tell.

Zhi Peng: I see your point. Good and evil exist in stories precisely because they are not real.

Fu Hsiang: That is correct. But this does not mean that we are not taken in by them. Our parents tell us fairy stories about bad people and their sticky end in order to encourage us to be good. We grow up with stories. In the Cultural Revolution, we grew up with stories about heroes of production. The Americans are in love with their own stories. Hollywood makes hundreds of stories about good guys and bad guys. The good guy is often American, the bad guy is often foreign – a terrorist. They fight and the good guy wins and the bad guy dies. Then the Americans go out into the real world to fight terrorists and they are hit by the paradoxical nature of good and evil.

Zhi Peng: But what about true stories? My father used to tell me stories about the Japanese – about what they did in Nanjing[11] for instance.

Fu Hsiang: True stories are not much different. Remember that the stories people tell are the product of their consciousness as well as their experience. Even a true story is not reality. It is that part of reality that that person experienced at that particular time, taken from its context and filtered through the nostalgia or repugnance of memory. You will get one description of what happened. The Rape of Nanjing is a collection of such stories taken from the people who survived. The event itself is not solid, it is passed to us as a snowstorm of experiences written and told by the people who lived through it.

Zhi Peng: Are you saying that their accounts are not accurate? That the Japanese didn't rape and murder thousands of Chinese?

Fu Hsiang: Their accounts are accurate as far they go. But they are not reality. Reality is something infinitely redescribable. And because it is infinitely redescribable, it cannot be properly described. This is what Lao Tse meant when he said that the Tao which is spoken is not the true Tao.[12]

Li Chen: I have heard a police friend say that when he breaks up a fight, he always gets different stories about who started it from different people.

Fu Hsiang: Naturally. This is part of the human condition.

Li Chen: *Sifu*, you said that people told stories and this was one reason they believed in the existence of evil, but you also said there was another. What is it?

Fu Hsiang: Time conspires against us in this matter. We experience ourselves as trapped in time. The present is clear and the past slopes away into the distance, but the future is clouded. People have all sorts of hopes and expectations about the future, but their knowledge is limited. This is why the I Ching[13] is consulted, not so that people can become wiser by its wisdom, but so that they peer through the mist of future time. So the full significance of events is lost to them. Once we lose sight of the nature of things, good and evil spring up like weeds.

Li Chen: Can you explain this to me?

Fu Hsiang: Look at the events we discussed yesterday; the extinction of the dinosaurs and the invasion of Tibet. Each event took place in a situation of terrible violence; the violence of nature in one and the violence of man in the other. To be at hand in either case would be to be appalled at the events unfolding. But to truly appreciate them in their full significance, you would need to stand master over time. To be able to see how each event was embedded in a larger unfolding, and how that unfolding, once understood, made judgments about good and evil impossible.

However, the nature of human consciousness is that it divides reality into past, present and future, and the future is obscure. Since our minds are limited by the present, judgments about good and evil appear.

Zhi Peng: *Sifu*, it seems to me that good and evil do exist, but they are mixed together. Things can be partly good and partly evil, just like a painting can be partly blue and partly red. Isn't this possible?

Fu Hsiang: It is certainly possible for a painting to be partly blue and partly red. But look at the events we described. What parts are good and what parts are evil? You cannot separate them at all. Without the destruction, there is no rebirth. The ancients who created the I Ching knew this, and in the tai chi symbol[14], the yin and the yang are joined into an inseparable whole.

Zhi Peng: This is true; we cannot separate out the good and the evil. It seems clear now.

Fu Hsiang: Clear to the enlightened mind certainly, but not to the unenlightened heart.   Men will always curse their ill-fortune and wish for better times, without realising that good and bad lie in their perception and not in the real world.

Li Chen: I must say that I am myself not much different in this regard. But how can we rise above our situation and liberate ourselves from this illusion?

Fu Hsiang: The liberation of the heart from good and evil begins with the philosophical recognition of their unreality.   From then on we need to root out our attachment to this illusion.

Li Chen: But how do we do this?

Fu Hsiang: Through meditation and reflection on the nature of our experience.   We have to carefully go through the events of our lives, and focus on the apparently evil events that befell us.   We start from the distant past and our earliest memories. In each case we have to reframe our description of what happened to break the hold of the old stories we told to ourselves. We tell ourselves new stories.   When we do this repeatedly, the heart lets go of past events and we are liberated from the illusion of evil. As we continue to do this, the heart follows the philosophical mind and eventually we learn to remain unattached when apparently evil things happen in the present. The heart is trained by the mind to tell itself that what is hurting it is an illusory part of a greater whole. When such non-attachment is present, much of the pain disappears.

Zhi Peng: Master, you said that there were three reasons why we believe in the objective existence of evil and you have only mentioned two; our telling stories and our experience of time. What is the third?

Fu Hsiang: Your memory does you credit, as does your persistence. Both qualities are needed for philosophical enquiry. The third reason is based on the relations between mind and action.

Zhi Peng: Please explain further.

Fu Hsiang: Action arises from intention. When we divine the motives of others, we often see that they are good or evil. When we do this, we then weigh the action and we judge it from the perspective of the intention that produced it. If the intention is evil, then we judge the action as evil. If the intention is good, we judge the action as good. In this way we transfer qualities of the internal world of the mind to the external world of the body.

We observe that certain dispositions produce certain actions. A man who is full of hate will naturally tend to be cruel and destructive. Hence we judge destructive events as if they were the product of evil intent. We naturally inclined to view these events themselves as evil, even when they are the product of impersonal forces.

Li Chen: My father used to swear that the bad things that happened were due to evil spirits in the house.

Fu Hsiang: True, although your father may not have been wrong in his belief. Such entities do exist.

Zhi Peng: Now I have a problem, *sifu*. You convinced me before that good and evil do not exist. Now you are telling me about evil spirits with a straight face. How can you maintain this position in the face of what you have already said?

Fu Hsiang: As regards evil spirits, this would take time to explain and perhaps you would not be ready for it.

Without the practical experience, my theorising can seem empty or even absurd. If you were being trained at Maoshan[15] then you would be expected to understand these matters. But if you find it hard to believe in evil spirits, then it should not be hard to believe in evil-spirited men, for there have been many such in history.

Zhi Peng: I can believe in evil men, to be sure. But I'm not sure that I can believe in evil men, and at the same time follow your teaching that good and evil are illusory.

Fu Hsiang: Good and evil are illusory when applied to the events of the external world. But it does not follow that they are illusory when they are applied to the soul. There are evil thoughts and evil intentions, just as there are good thoughts and good intentions. In general we can say that good and evil are properly found in the world of properties and in the workings of the mind. We can say justice or compassion are good, and we can say that cruelty and treachery are bad. We can say that such and such an intention was noble or ignoble. All these statements make sense.

Zhi Peng: I follow your distinction, but I do not understand why you make it. Why is the mind set aside from your previous arguments? Why is it possible for our intentions to be evil when you deny the existence of evil elsewhere?

Fu Hsiang: Intentions have a special property that external events do not have. We cannot say that a physical event like the invasion of Tibet is good or evil because as soon as we do so, we can find a description under which it appears in the contrary light. But intentions are often not like that.

Zhi Peng: Can you give an example?

Fu Hsiang: We can take the invasion of Tibet itself. When Mao defeated the armies of Chiang Kai-shek in 1949, he took control of China. Once he had control, he realised that he had the power to take Tibet, which was weakly defended and no match for his armies. So he annexed Tibet and captured great territories for China. There was little noble about what he did. His aim was totally aggressive and was executed with no regard for the wishes of the Tibetans themselves. We can say that Mao intended a brutal seizure of Tibet in 1950 and this is exactly what happened. Now it is also true that that brutal seizure of Tibet in 1950 is one and the same with the event that brought Tibetan Buddhism to the West. But Mao did not intend to disseminate Tibetan Buddhism to the West! I'm sure he would be dismayed at the thought that his invasion disseminated a culture that he did his best to stamp out.

Li Chen: He certainly did; many scrolls were destroyed and monasteries were burnt to the ground.

Fu Hsiang: Intentions are rather like stories themselves. When we resolve to do something, gain a promotion, win honour, conquer a country, we frame a story to ourselves. This story is a story of how great things will be if we accomplish our dream. Being a story it is incomplete and lacks detail, and in our story we may seem like heroes. Of course our motives may be totally unworthy. The difference between a daydream and an intention is that a daydream stays as a story; but a genuine intention is put into effect. If we genuinely intend something, we try to make the story come true. If we are successful, then it does become true.

Li Chen: And what happens then?

Fu Hsiang: It becomes part of reality, and when it does, it loses its story-like quality and becomes indescribable and many-sided. It acquires qualities it never had when it was just a story. It can trap us and devour us if we are not careful. The old story tellers knew this; that is why there are folk tales about spirits who grant three wishes to people. Often people feel worse off when their wishes come true than if they had never wished at all.

Li Chen, you look troubled.

Li Chen: Master, I am troubled. You have taught me that good and evil are unreal, but as a Buddhist I have been taught to do good. What can I make of your teaching as a Buddhist?

Fu Hsiang: This is too large a topic to discuss in one sitting. We need to rest our minds as well as our bodies. We will speak on this tomorrow.

The Third Discourse

The Paradox of the Good and the Wise

Fu Hsiang: Your form is improving, soon we will be able to move to the smaller circle[16] in your exercises.

Li Chen: Thank you master. Master, yesterday I asked you how it was possible for me to remain a Buddhist and believe in what you are teaching.

Fu Hsiang: There are many kinds of Buddhist. Perhaps you cannot remain the Buddhist you are and learn from me. But perhaps you can become a different kind of Buddhist.

Li Chen: At the moment I am no kind of Buddhist at all. My mind keeps asking me "Why be good, because goodness is an illusion." And I have no answer.

Fu Hsiang: It is a question that has troubled some great minds. Philosophers have thought, since they could not locate goodness in the external world, that talking of things as good or evil was senseless; like the lowing of cows or the bleating of sheep[17]. Others have said that such remarks are only ways of describing how one feels[18] or a way of commanding others[19].

Li Chen: I do not want to join their ranks, to be sure. But my mind keeps revolving on this question.

Fu Hsiang: Such puzzlement is like a fever.

Li Chen: In what way?

Fu Hsiang: You know that when a man has fever, he struggles and his temperature rises. Just before his fever breaks, his anguish is at its height and he rolls about and pours sweat.   The body expels the negative qi[20] as heat.   This crisis is followed by cooling and calm as the body restores its natural order.

In a similar way, when we take the medicine of philosophy to expel ignorance from our minds, we are at first confused.   Our anguish grows as our familiar ideas fall away one by one.   Soon we are in crisis. But when we finally arrive at the understanding provided by philosophy, then our crisis ends.   Our minds become cool and collected and we revert to our original nature.

Li Chen: I think I must have reached my crisis already. I am so confused in my mind.

Fu Hsiang: You have a way to go yet before your mind is clear. Would you prefer to end these discourses and learn only *bagua*?

Zhi Peng: For myself *sifu*, I must say that I look forward to these discourses as much as I enjoy learning *bagua*. But I am not a Buddhist, and so I do not feel as badly as my friend.

Li Chen: I feel I cannot stay as I am. Since I have begun taking your medicine, I must finish the course.

Fu Hsiang: Well then. Let us examine the problem. Can you intend the impossible?

Li Chen: I am sorry, *sifu*. What do you mean?

Fu Hsiang: What I mean is; can you intend to do something that you honestly believe you cannot do. For instance, you believe that you cannot jump sixty *chi* [21]into the air.

Li Chen: Of course not. That is impossible.

Fu Hsiang: So believing that this is impossible, you cannot truly intend to jump sixty *chi* into the air.

Li Chen: That's right.

Fu Hsiang: And there are many other things you believe you cannot do. For instance, you believe that you cannot lift one thousand *jin*[22] or make yourself invisible or be suddenly rich in one second and many other things of this kind.

Li Chen: None of these things are possible.

Fu Hsiang: So being impossible in your eyes, you cannot have any intention to lift one thousand *jin* or make yourself invisible.

Li Chen: Of course not, to try to do any of these things would be absurd.

Zhi Peng: I think it is clear *sifu*, what you meant by your question and what the answer should be. You cannot intend to do what you believe is impossible.

Li Chen: I understand now; yes, that is correct.

Fu Hsiang: You would certainly be unwise to try to do these things. But in the light of our previous conversations about good and evil, could one be truly wise and still believe in the existence of good and evil?

Li Chen: Certainly you could not be called wise if you continued to believe that good and evil are properties of external events and objects.

Fu Hsiang: Moreover we established that, viewed as events in themselves, actions were neither good nor evil. As soon as we bring our intentions into being, they acquire the paradoxical features that all things acquire when they are part of the Tao.

Li Chen: We arrived at this conclusion.

Fu Hsiang: So a wise man must believe that he cannot do good, since by our account, he believes that goodness and evil do not reside in the events of the external world. Consequently he cannot intend to perform good acts.

Li Chen: My head swims and I feel more uncomfortable than ever. But I must assent to your reasoning.

Fu Hsiang: But can a man be described as good if he never intends to do good?

Li Chen: It seems impossible, I must confess.

Fu Hsiang: Therefore, we must conclude that goodness and wisdom cannot be found together, and the wise man cannot be good.

Li Chen: This gets worse!   *Sifu*, I feel quite ill and the fever you spoke of is now even stronger.   When I arrived my mind was not at peace, but revolved endlessly around the questions that our conversations produced.   But now I feel like a man who has been bound so tightly that he cannot even wiggle his toes.

Zhi Peng: Even I am not easy with our conclusions.   In China, we have often followed Confucius who advocated good behaviour and was venerated as one of the wise men of his time.   But now it seems that goodness and wisdom are forever separate, and we were wrong to believe that Confucius was wise.

Fu Hsiang: Well, if our friend is bound so tightly that he cannot even wiggle his toes, we must try to release him.   However, the knot in this case is large and complex. If we are to untie you, we need you to be patient while we unravel the knot. You know in these cases, sometimes one has to perform many strange maneuvers to release a person from being tied up. At first he seems to be unaffected by your actions, but then suddenly, he finds that the knot falls apart and he is free. But if he loses patience with elaborate motions and struggles to free himself by force, then he ends up more tightly bound than before.

Li Chen: You may rely on me to keep my patience until the knot is untied. Even if our discourse takes us to strange places, I shall not give up, but I will follow the motions of your mind.

Zhi Peng: And I too.

Fu Hsiang: Well spoken, for patience and courage are the qualities we need in pursuit of true philosophy. Nor must we refrain from accepting a conclusion if calm and clear reason delivers it to us. You are both prepared to follow the argument to its destination. Let us meet again after the next lesson to continue our investigations.

The Fourth Discourse

The Inferior Man, the Superior Man and the Sage

Zhi Peng: *Sifu*, in the last lesson you formulated a paradox which seems to have no solution. I cannot fault the reasoning, but I cannot bring myself to accept the conclusion, which is that good people are fools.

Fu Hsiang: 'Fools' is perhaps a little harsh. Remember people once believed that the sun went round the earth and that the earth was flat. They were not fools. To judge incorrectly does not make one a fool.

Zhi Peng: Nevertheless, I would like to know more of your teaching on this matter.

Fu Hsiang: Very well. But to understand the solution to the paradox, we have to investigate human nature.

Zhi Peng: I am ready to learn.

Fu Hsiang: You have grown up during communism in China and now you are living through capitalism. Have you noticed the changes happening in China now?

Zhi Peng: Nobody can fail to miss them. All around the old is making way for the new. Buildings are torn down and new ones are put in their place. Factories are being built and roads are widened and improved. People are leaving the countryside and making their way to cities to get jobs. China is changing every day.

Fu Hsiang: Everything you say is true. But what of the people themselves? How do they compare to the people you knew when you were a child?

Zhi Peng: They are different too. In the old days everybody read the thoughts of Chairman Mao. There were worker's meetings everywhere, and people discussed only the revolution. They worked hard for Communism and they had ideals. Now people are only interested in making money. They are selfish and think only of themselves. The children are not respectful as they once were. The one child policy[23] has produced a nation of little emperors who are spoilt. If we are not careful we will end up like the Americans who care only for money.

Fu Hsiang: This is how the majority of human beings have been throughout history. The inferior man's thoughts are never far from his belly. He is driven by desires for material things. He is like that American cartoon character we are always watching.

Li Chen: Homer Simpson?

Zhi Peng: Homer Simpson is perfect for capitalism don't you think? He is the product of American advertising. He is what the advertising men are pushing the Americans to become. No sooner does he see an advertisement for something than he wants it. He does not think unless it is needed to satisfy his desires, and then he does not think clearly or well. His body is fat and stuffed with junk food and his brain is full of TV.

Li Chen: I like Homer Simpson, but it is true that I would not like to be like him.

Fu Hsiang: Our own peasants are not so different in their hearts, Li Chen. If you could look into their dreams, you would find that they wanted many of the things that Homer has got. And if they got these things, many of them would behave in just the same way as Homer. They are thin because they cannot afford rich American food, and they are healthy because they have to do physical work in order to live. But given a choice they would abandon these things and live like Homer.

Li Chen: You are right, it is depressing to contemplate it. Most people are not interested in the virtuous life. Even our intelligentsia is obsessed with self-promotion.

Zhi Peng: That's right. When I was at university I could see that the professors were not interested in the students. All they wanted to do was publish as many papers as possible, so as to advance in their careers. Money and position were their twin concerns and whatever they did was aimed at their own advantage. So many of those papers were repetitious, but as long as they made up the numbers it did not matter. These professors were not true scholars, because for them their profession was only a means of advancing their interests.

Li Chen: But not everybody is like that. Many of my Buddhist friends devote many hours of their spare time to helping people. They visit the sick and give time and money to good works. I remember that some of my professors devoted a lot of time to their students.

Fu Hsiang: In what way are these people different?

Li Chen: These people had principles by which they lived. They had an idea of right and wrong and they tried to live by the right, even if it did not benefit them.

Fu Hsiang: Even if they have not read his work, these people live by the ideals of Confucius. They devote themselves to service. They are indeed more evolved than the people who serve only themselves. We can say that they are superior men and women. They have a moral code and they try to live up to it. So we have two classes of people; the inferior person who serves himself and the superior person, who lives by a moral code and tries to do good in helping others.

Li Chen: This is true, and there can be no other category. Even though, from what we have said before, the superior man is lacking in true wisdom since goodness is an illusion.

Fu Hsiang: But there is one more category left.

Li Chen: What is it?

Fu Hsiang: It is a category that is thinly populated in present times and in history. But it has included some of the greatest men and women who have walked this earth. It is the category of the enlightened philosopher or sage.[24]

Li Chen: What is the difference between the sage and the superior man?

Fu Hsiang: The sage sees the essential nature of things and recognises that good and evil are illusory, but nevertheless performs good acts.

Zhi Peng: Master, surely our reasoning has established that it is impossible to be both good and wise. How can there be a sage?

Fu Hsiang: The sage produces good acts in the same way that a fire produces sparks. It arises from his essential nature.

Zhi Peng: I confess that I still do not understand.

Fu Hsiang: Have you ever seen a child at play?

Zhi Peng: Of course.

Fu Hsiang: Then if you see a child at play, in complete joy and abandon, you will see his essential nature displayed.   His movements are not calculated, there is no end in sight.   He does not aim to please or be successful.   His movements are the product of an overwhelming energy and not intent.

In contrast, the movements of an adult are controlled by his mind. If you see an adult playing a game, he is controlled. Every action is measured by his intention.

Li Chen: You are saying that a sage is like a child?

Fu Hsiang: Yes, in that his actions are spontaneous and unrehearsed.   But while a child is spontaneous, he is also ignorant of the essential nature of things.   The sage is cognisant of the nature of things; he correctly perceives that both good and evil are illusory, but his nature is like that of a child.   Since he acts without intent, he transcends the paradox. He is both good and wise.

Zhi Peng: I understand what you are saying *sifu*, but I don't think I have ever known such a person. Nor do I think that such a person should be placed above the superior man. If a person did good because he was a sage, it would only be because he had the good fortune to be born with a good character.   But the superior man who does what is right because it is right, rises above his character to do good and should be more admired for that very reason.[25]

Fu Hsiang: You suppose that we acquire the character of a sage from birth as a gift.   But not so; to recover our essential natures requires hard work and diligence.

Li Chen: I understand the master's ideas, but I am still lost.

Fu Hsiang: Why is that?

Li Chen: Well, I am not a sage.   So even if the sage can do good while knowing that goodness is an illusion, I cannot.   I still have no reason for being good and so no reason for being a Buddhist.

Fu Hsiang: Tell me, have you ever hurt yourself?   For example, have you ever strained a muscle or broken your arm or leg?

Li Chen: Yes, when I was a boy I had a fall from the roof of our house and broke my arm.

41

Fu Hsiang: And how were you treated?

Li Chen: My arm was put in plaster and I had a sling. Later the plaster was removed and I had to do exercises.

Fu Hsiang: You did exercises because your arm was weak?

Li Chen: That's right.

Fu Hsiang: You did not have the proper use of your arm. So to regain it, you did exercise. This is true of human beings in general; that when a faculty is strong, then we use it and when a faculty is weak, we make it strong by trying to use it.

Li Chen: Could you explain this?

Fu Hsiang: The way you were treated for your broken arm is the way that we cultivate our weakest faculties. For example if we are naturally inclined to be selfish, then we cultivate generosity by being generous. At first this is an effort, but gradually it becomes habitual and we eliminate our selfish nature. If we lack physical courage, we can gain it by setting ourselves physical challenges until we eliminate our cowardice.

Li Chen: I understand.

Fu Hsiang: We cannot leap from being inferior men to being sages. We need to walk a path to become sages and part of that path will first make us superior people. But if we become superior people whilst under the influence of philosophy, while correctly perceiving the illusory nature of good and evil, we shall be much stronger and more resilient than the superior men who live today.

Li Chen: In what way?

Fu Hsiang: The unenlightened superior man believes in the existence of good and evil. He tries to do good and make a better world. Yet the unpredictable nature of the world means his designs are often frustrated. Friends let him down; money meant for a good cause is embezzled and squandered. Corruption gets in the way of the noblest project. When the superior man encounters these things, he is dismayed in his heart. He feels his failure keenly and blames those around him. In this way, the noblest natures are apt to fall into bitterness when confronted with the reality of the world and the schemes of inferior men.

In contrast, the superior man who is on a conscious journey to become a sage, begins his journey with the understanding that good and evil are illusory and that his good acts are only a means to an end. He proceeds by acting like a sage, doing right, but separating himself from the fruit of his action. He recognises correctly that the results of his actions are of less importance than the intent behind them. Since he does not trouble himself with the events of the world, he avoids bitterness and pain.

Li Chen: I see what you mean now. *Sifu*, I believe my fever is over. You are saying it is possible for me to embrace the eightfold path and yet deny the existence of good and evil as objective properties of events.

Fu Hsiang: It seems your fever is broken. Like every good doctor, I end my clinic when the patient is cured. I shall meet you both at the same time tomorrow.

The Fifth Discourse

The Essential Nature of Human Beings

Zhi Peng: *Sifu*, I have been reading Hun Tzu[26] and he says that the essential nature of man is evil. On the other hand, I have heard Taoists say that our essential nature is good. What do you think?

Li Chen: Is this question important? Since we are bound to behave as superior men, and follow the eightfold path, does it matter from where we begin?

Fu Hsiang: It is important because depending on how we answer Zhi's question, we shall arrange the education of our children differently. If we think that their essential nature is evil, then we will seek to control them from their earliest years. We shall watch them as carefully as wild animals, and curb every evil tendency as soon as it appears. Our motto shall be "Vigilance and discipline". If we think that they are essentially good, then we will seek to release their goodness in the same way that a good sculptor releases a statue from marble; by following the natural lines of the character. Accordingly our training will be light and directed at guiding the natural growth of the child as a good gardener, only binding the plant so that it grows more directly to the sun.

Zhi Peng: So *sifu*, what do you think? Are we essentially good or evil?

Fu Hsiang: I have taught you both esoteric anatomy,[27] what are the principal organs of the body?

Zhi Peng: The ten principal organs are the kidneys, the liver, the lungs, the large intestines, the bladder, the small intestines, the heart, the stomach, the spleen and the gall bladder.

Fu Hsiang: How are these organs associated with each other?

Li Chen: The organs are paired with each other, yin and yang[28]; the kidneys with the bladder, the spleen with the stomach, the liver is paired with the gall bladder, the lungs with the large intestine and the heart is paired with the small intestine.

Fu Hsiang: Excellent. And who can tell me the afflictive emotions and which organs they affect?

Zhi Peng: The five afflictive emotions are fear, anger, grief, hysteria, and worry. Fear affects the kidneys and the bladder, worry affects the stomach and the spleen, grief affects the large intestine and the lungs, hysteria affects the heart and small intestine and anger affects the liver and gall bladder.[29]

Fu Hsiang: If the soul is afflicted with any of these negative emotions then the corresponding organs will be affected. If these emotions are held for any period, then illness will appear. What kind of afflictions may appear in the body if the soul is afflicted with fear?

Li Chen: Sexual impotency, lumbar pain and weakness in the legs.

Fu Hsiang: And how will the person behave who is afflicted with fear?

Li Chen: He cannot be relied upon, but will act as a coward when called upon to be brave. Hence he will be unreliable and perhaps treacherous.

Fu Hsiang: And acts of treachery and cowardice are ignoble?

Li Chen: Most definitely.

Fu Hsiang: Suppose that he is afflicted with anger? What signs might we expect to see in the body?

Li Chen: Pains in the liver and gallstones.

Fu Hsiang: And how will he behave?

Li Chen: He will be a terror to those close to him. Sparing nobody the lash of his tongue, he will be addicted to destructive acts and wanton violence.

Fu Hsiang: These are certainly not the characteristics of the virtuous man. What of the person who is lost in grief? What signs both physical and mental would we expect to see?

Li Chen: Weakness in the lungs. Possibly chronic colds or tuberculosis. Problems with excretion such as constipation or irritable bowel. As a character, he is prone to depression and mourning. Feeling that his life is empty, he is hard to rouse to action.

Fu Hsiang: What of the man who is prone to hysteria?

Li Chen: He may suffer a heart attack. In character, he is voluble and excitable, full of grand schemes and grand ideas which amount to little. He may impress the gullible, but his speeches have no real substance and so he misleads those who follow him.

Fu Hsiang: And what of the worrier?

Li Chen: Stomach ulcers are common with him and cancer, since the spleen controls the immune system and the immune system fights cancer. In life he is obsessive over detail, continually nit-picking over the same items again and again and spending energy on trifles. He is a distraction to work with and a burden to his colleagues.

Fu Hsiang: When we see evil intentions arise in another, do we not see that behind these intentions is one or more of these afflictive emotions? When a man seeks to inflict pain on another, do we not find within his soul, the marks of cruelty and anger? When the chief advisor Qin Hui condemned Marshal Yueh Fei to death, was it not because of fear of the general's popularity[30]?

Li Chen: Yes, it is true. Evil intent is like a tree and the seeds of that tree are the afflictive emotions.

Fu Hsiang: Well spoken. Indeed, evil intentions and evil actions are the fruit of the seed that is the afflictive emotions. But the afflictive emotions are also the seed of many physical illnesses too. So we see that they bear a double harvest, both in the soul and in the body.

Zhi Peng: *Sifu*, I follow what you are saying, but I cannot see its relevance to my question.

Fu Hsiang: You asked whether men are essentially good or evil. Tell me, Zhi Peng, would you feed hamburgers to a horse?

Zhi Peng: *Sifu*, your questions are stranger and stranger! Why would I feed hamburgers to a horse?

Fu Hsiang: Bear with my questions; why would you not do so?

Zhi Peng: Horses do not eat hamburgers.

Fu Hsiang: Well suppose we were to make the horse eat hamburgers and only hamburgers. What would happen?

Zhi Peng: Well, if we could get the horse to eat them, it would become sick. The digestive system of a horse is not designed for meat.

Fu Hsiang: You are saying that the horse is essentially vegetarian?

Zhi Peng: Yes, that's right.

Fu Hsiang: You are saying that the horse is essentially vegetarian because, if we force it away from the vegetarian diet, it becomes ill.

Zhi Peng: That seems a reasonable way of putting it.

Fu Hsiang: We also agreed that evil action arises from evil intent, and that evil intent arises from afflictive emotion.

Zhi Peng: We did.

Fu Hsiang: Moreover we said that afflictive emotion creates illness.

Zhi Peng: True.

Fu Hsiang: So we can say that if a man deviates from the virtuous life, he is prey to illness. Therefore in just the same way that we concluded a horse is essentially vegetarian, we must conclude that man is essentially virtuous.

Zhi Peng: I now see the line of your reasoning, *sifu*. The conclusion seems inescapable, I must say. I did not see it before.

Fu Hsiang: Since we are essentially virtuous beings, the negative emotions that nurture evil also harm our bodies. They make us repulsive to our own kind and condemn us to loneliness and fear. But the contrary emotions of courage, love, kindness and forgiveness all nourish our bodies, increase our longevity and make us attractive to others.

Zhi Peng: Master, you have answered my question completely. Our essence is goodness. But now I have another question.

Fu Hsiang: What is it?

Zhi Peng: If people are essentially good, why do they commit so much evil?

Fu Hsiang: Zhi Peng, you have asked one of the deepest questions. If you are willing to continue this discourse, we will see what we can make of this in your next lesson.

The Sixth Discourse

Li Chen and Zhi Peng Debate the Origin of Evil

Scene: *the park of the Heavenly Temple. In a grotto of trees, Zhi Peng and Li Chen are performing pa kua under the watchful eyes of Master Hsiang.*

Fu Hsiang: Relaxation is the key to the internal arts. Your movement must be relaxed in that the *qi* may itself move through the body. Remember that the body of the true martial artist is 'steel wrapped in cotton',[31] not cotton wrapped in steel. Both of you need to relax and sink your energy into the *dan tien.*[32]

Zhi Peng: It is hard to truly relax when one's mind is focused on what one is doing.

Fu Hsiang: You have been practicing now for two hours. Time, I think to relax. You can stop now.

Zhi Peng: Thank you, master. Master, in the last lesson we discussed the nature of man and we concluded that men were essentially good. But now I wish to know why it is that they are often evil.

Fu Hsiang: So you wish to travel to the well, but you want me to draw the water.

Zhi Peng: Master?

Fu Hsiang: One day, Zhi Peng, I will not be with you, and then others will come to you and ask questions. If you cannot travel to the well of truth yourself, and draw the water, how will you be able to answer them?

Zhi Peng: Master, I am sorry. I did not mean to offend you.

Fu Hsiang: I am not offended. But there is a skill for you to learn, of being able to answer questions as well as ask them.

Zhi Peng: In this case, I feel my answers will be inadequate.

Fu Hsiang: We should feel no shame at being wrong in our answers. The only cause for shame is in not attempting to answer at all. You have already proved yourself worthy by asking a good question. You prove yourself doubly worthy by trying to answer it. But you are not alone, for your friend is interested in the answer himself.

Li Chen: That is true.

Zhi Peng: Very well. I should say that there are many reasons why men become evil. For instance, we may be born to bad parents, who do not bring us up correctly, but practice all kinds of vices and beat us. We may be visited by disease or lose all our possessions in war or flood. These things embitter and twist people, and force them to all kinds of desperate acts.

Fu Hsiang: Very good; a sensible answer. You would not mind if we examine it?

Zhi Peng: Of course not.

Fu Hsiang: If I have a piece of purest gold, how many times must I strike it in order to turn it to lead?

Li Chen: You cannot turn gold into lead by striking it, *sifu*. No matter how many times you strike it, it still remains gold.

Fu Hsiang: And if I heat it, or melt it and cut it into a thousand pieces?

Li Chen: It still remains gold throughout.

Fu Hsiang: So if a man's essential nature is pure gold, could apparent misfortune turn it to lead?

Li Chen: It is difficult to see how it could.

Fu Hsiang: Here is another thought. We argued that external events were neither good nor evil.

Li Chen: We did.

Fu Hsiang: Now if an external event was such that it inevitably produced an evil person, wouldn't it be evil itself? For example, if a hard childhood with a drunken father inevitably, and in every case, produced a bad character, wouldn't that show that such an upbringing was evil in itself?

Li Chen: It would be hard to say that in such a case, this upbringing was not itself evil, since it would invariably produce evil in the soul.

Fu Hsiang: But in fact, we have established already, that external events are not themselves good or evil, and hence we cannot argue that such an upbringing is itself evil.

Li Chen: Such a conclusion is not open to us.

Fu Hsiang: In fact, do we not find that those with hard childhoods, may also turn out as loving and indulgent parents; not wishing the pains of their past childhood to be inflicted on their own children?

Li Chen: This does happen.

Fu Hsiang: So we must conclude from our reasoning, that circumstance and upbringing do not dictate the development of character. Hence humans must possess a degree of free will to separate themselves from their situation.

Li Chen: This does follow from what we agreed.

Fu Hsiang: So if a man's character is purest gold, and his essential nature is untainted, circumstance can never produce an evil disposition in him. On the contrary, the darkness of the troubled world will only cause his light to shine more brightly. But what if his character is not pure? Will the things of which Zhi Peng has spoken have an effect?

Li Chen: It is likely they would.

Fu Hsiang: If we have not pure gold, but a mixture of gold and lead. If we heat it wrongly and throw away the wrong part, can we not increase the amount of lead and diminish the amount of gold and so reduce the value of the thing itself?

Li Chen: This is quite possible.

Fu Hsiang: So it would seem that Zhi's explanation is like that; in that it explains how a man who is a mixture of lead and gold can lose his gold and become leaden, but it cannot explain how a man of pure gold can acquire lead.

Li Chen: Yes, that is right.

Zhi Peng: Well I'll agree my answer was not altogether satisfactory. But can you do any better?

Li Chen: In Buddhism, we are taught that our character depends on our desires and our past *karma*, which is nothing more than the fruits of previous lifetimes.

Zhi Peng: Well, that theory seems no better than mine. If a man's evil characteristics are inherited from the evil he committed in a previous life, then this simply pushes the question back. From where did he inherit the corruption of that life?

Li Chen: Perhaps from the one before that. Perhaps there are an infinite number of such lives.

Zhi Peng: Such a view is not consistent with what we know of the age of this planet and the universe itself. Besides, what sense is there in saying that men are essentially good if you are going to say that they have been corrupted for an eternity of time and there was never a time in which they were purely good?

Li Chen: I take your point. Well, though the Buddha himself was a perfectly realised being, my teachers tell that he was tempted by the demon Mara while he was meditating under the *bo* tree.   Such beings could be the origin of the corruption.

Zhi Peng: How can you tempt a person who is incorruptible?   If a being is perfected and good, how can he or she fall into evil?   The point of the story was that Buddha resisted the demon because of his perfection, which guaranteed him from harm.   If we are pure gold, how can we be corrupted?

Li Chen: I must admit that none of the answers either of us have given seem to answer the question, but I have no more answers to give.

Zhi Peng: Nor I.   Master, we have drawn from the well, but our buckets are empty.

Fu Hsiang: Not altogether. You have at least found out some answers which are insufficient, and in the course of doing so, you have exercised your minds as well as your bodies.   But this time I must be the one to leave, for I have an appointment on the other side of the city.

The Seventh Discourse

The Will to Power and the Formation of the Self

Zhi Peng: Master, last time we argued the origin of evil but could not arrive at any satisfactory conclusion.

Fu Hsiang: The reasons you both gave were not in themselves incorrect. Bad conditions can worsen an already flawed character, and karma can visit misfortune upon a person. But it is true that there is something missing from these accounts. The problem, as you both saw, was how to explain the original corruption. This problem has occupied the attention of thinkers for a long time. It is not likely that we can find the root without patient examination on the origins and development of human beings. Do you really wish to pursue this quarry wherever it may run?

Zhi Peng: Master, I feel we must hunt down the solution wherever the argument takes us.

Li Chen: I agree.

Fu Hsiang: Well, since you are unanimous, perhaps we should begin with a very old answer. In the Bible of the Christians, the book of Genesis begins with an account of how men came to be corrupted.

Zhi Peng: You mean the Fall?

Fu Hsiang: Remind me of how it goes.

Zhi Peng: Adam and Eve are the first humans and they live in the Garden of Eden which is a paradise. However the garden has a snake or tempter. The snake corrupts Eve by persuading her to eat of the apple of the Tree of Knowledge. Once corrupted, she in turn tempts Adam and he eats the apple and is corrupted too. The Christian God is angry and expels them from the garden.

Fu Hsiang: It is a strange story. But we all inhabited such a garden at one time in this very life.

Li Chen: Where is it?

Fu Hsiang: Think. At what part of your life were you blissful, your every need was provided for and you did not have to struggle for sustenance?

Li Chen: When I was small?

Fu Hsiang: Even when you were small, you had to obey your parents. There were duties and obligations. The life of a child is not always blissful. No, this garden in which you lived supplied your every need and you lived in it. But finally, after nine months, you were expelled from it to make your way in the world.

Li Chen: Master, you are talking of the womb.

Fu Hsiang: I am. In the womb, we float suspended in the mother's fluids. We take our nutrition through our *dan tien* via the umbilical cord. The unborn child breathes in the manner of a Taoist master. It is immortal; its prenatal energy is untouched. But as soon as it is born, it separates itself from the mother and begins the evolution towards adulthood and death. As it grows, it accumulates more energy from food and the air and the light of this world. Eventually at one score years and eight, he or she reaches their peak of development.

Li Chen: And then?

Fu Hsiang: From the age of twenty eight we begin to decline. The accumulation of poisonous chemicals, toxic thoughts and emotions, bad food, drinking, child birth, menstruation, indiscriminate sex, disease and poor breathing begin to tell. Year by year our store of *qi* declines, our skin sags and our hair falls out until the prenatal *qi* with which we are born is finally exhausted. At that point death closes in and we are carried out of incarnation.

Li Chen: This is certainly life as you have described it; even if it is rather depressing to recount it.

Fu Hsiang: But our interests lie at a much earlier stage; for we are trying to locate the point of corruption. Is it likely that we are corrupted in the womb?

Li Chen: It is hard to see how we could be.

Fu Hsiang: Then the process must begin after birth. If we look at a new born baby, how does it behave?

Li Chen: Well it cries.

Fu Hsiang: True, it may do. But how does it move its body?

Li Chen: The new born baby has no control over its body. It cannot focus its eyes or keep its head steady, its arms and legs wave about randomly.

Fu Hsiang: That is correct. For the new born child, its limbs and the whole of its body are not under its control. There is no distinction between the world of its own body and the world outside of its body. Both are mysterious and unpredictable. So what is the new born's first task?

Li Chen: It must be to take command of its own body.

Fu Hsiang: The first organs that it will master are the eyes. It will be able to focus and move its eyes to look upon objects which interest it. Then it masters the art of turning its head. Next it learns to move its arms and grasp objects. Finally it learns to crawl and then walk.

Li Chen: This is the natural pattern of development certainly.

Fu Hsiang: These tasks are not easy. What can we say about the will of the new born baby in the light of these accomplishments?

Li Chen: Certainly it must be self-willed to a great degree.

Fu Hsiang: Every healthy human being is born with the will to power, and the territory he first sets out to conquer is his own body.   But at birth, the baby has no clear conception of his body as an entity separate from the rest of the world. He simply sets out to dominate without having any idea of what is within his power and what is not.   What do you suppose would happen if the baby did not have that will to power?

Li Chen: It is difficult to see how a baby could progress and develop if it simply lay in its crib and watched the world go by.

Fu Hsiang: There are babies who are like that; who are extremely passive towards their environment.   They display little interest in anything and are slow to develop. In the natural course of things, these babies die and do not make it to childhood.

Li Chen: That would seem to be their fate, unless they are given the most intensive care.

Fu Hsiang: So we must disagree with those philosophers who have thought that a new born baby is simply a recording device like a camera, accepting input from the senses and retaining it.[33] On the contrary, the first impulse is towards power and control.

Li Chen: So it would seem.

Fu Hsiang: So the new born child embarks on a journey of conquest, not knowing what is possible and what is not, but trying to control everything within his grasp.

Li Chen: That is correct.

Fu Hsiang: Now, let us imagine, just for a moment, that the baby was omnipotent. That is to say, there is no limit to what it can do. Whatever it desires is immediately manifested and whatever it dislikes is banished.

Zhi Peng: This would be a very unusual baby, *sifu*. I'm not sure that the world would be a safe place if there was such a child.

Fu Hsiang: I would agree that it is fortunate for us that there is no such child. But my next question is hypothetical.

Zhi Peng: What is it?

Fu Hsiang: Assuming there was such a child, it could manipulate the stuff of the material world as easily as its own imagination. Walls and buildings would be no obstacle to it. Everything would be a toy of its all-powerful mind. Now for such a child, what could lead it to form the idea of the world as something separate from itself?

Zhi Peng: In such a case, it would be very difficult for the child to truly believe in the existence of an external world apart from his desires. For what we call the real world would be, to him, as malleable as any phantasm of the mind.

Fu Hsiang: In fact, if the child's ability to control his body at will is what makes him say this is *his* body, then since he can control everything at whim, will he not see everything as part of himself?

Zhi Peng: Yes he would.

Fu Hsiang: But since everything is perceived as part of himself, does the concept of *himself* have any meaning for him? Since there is nothing that is not him, what sense is there to *not-him* and hence what sense is there to *him*?

Zhi Peng: Since there is no contrast to *him* in his mind, there is no sense of *him* either in his mind.

Fu Hsiang: Just so; a child who is born with the will to power and who is gifted or cursed with omnipotence cannot form an idea of self and thus cannot become self-conscious.

Zhi Peng: That would seem logical.

Fu Hsiang: So logically again, since children do attain self-consciousness, this must arise from the interaction between their will to power and their lack of omnipotence.

Zhi Peng: Correct.

Fu Hsiang: What we suppose then, is that the child born with the will to power embarks on his path of conquest and fairly quickly learns to control his body.

But when it comes to the control of his mother and father, he learns that these objects cannot be controlled to his satisfaction and the perimeter of his little empire marks his sphere of control. Within the perimeter is what he calls *himself* and what lies outside that perimeter is not-*himself.*

Zhi Peng: I agree.

Fu Hsiang: So we have established the conditions and manner under which the new born child establishes self-consciousness. We have strained our minds enough for today and it is time to exercise the body. Now for some *bagua.*

The Eighth Discourse

The Formation of the Afflictive Emotions

Zhi Peng: Master, could we continue from the point of our last conversation?

Fu Hsiang: Remind me, at what point we had arrived in our last conversation. It is several days since we last met.

Zhi Peng: We began with tracing the development of a human being, and the existence of the will to power. From that point we established that the interaction of the will to power and the experience of powerlessness gave rise to the idea of self.

Fu Hsiang: Now I am reminded. That is correct; the child expands his domain of his power until he eventually meets a check. That check occurs when what he wishes to happen, or desires to possess, does not happen or does not fall within his possession. You have children?

Li Chen: As you know *sifu*, one girl and one boy.

Fu Hsiang: Then you know how very small children behave when they want something, but are denied it.

Li Chen: Only too well, *sifu*. They kick up the most awful squall.

Fu Hsiang: Exactly so; a tantrum. Such behaviour is common at the age of two, when the child first comes to terms with the perimeter of the self. No longer are his wishes granted by merely having to bawl. It is at this age that the child comes to terms with his lack of power. It is from this age that we date our earliest memories and it is from this age that we become conscious of ourselves. Parents have even given this period a name; the 'terrible twos'.

Li Chen: It is certainly a trying time, even from my own memories as a parent.

Fu Hsiang: The child has experienced one of the primary afflictive emotions.

Li Chen: You mean anger?

Fu Hsiang: Exactly. Anger arises when that which we desire is denied to us. But it is not the only afflictive emotion. What happens if you take away something from a child as a punishment? For example, you take an ice-cream away from him when he is naughty; what happens then?

Li Chen: Well, you had better stop your ears in that case. The child will scream and wail.

Fu Hsiang: Now the child experiences the second primary afflictive emotion, which is grief. But suppose you try this experiment. You only appear to the child, when the child is enjoying a sweet and then you take it away. Your every appearance is accompanied by the plain theft of something he is enjoying. What do you think the child would feel when you appear to his sight?

Li Chen: Great apprehension, I would imagine; together with the original emotions that you inspired in him.

Fu Hsiang: Just so, the child experiences his previous emotions plus the third and final primary emotion, which is fear. Fear is the emotion that arises from the expectation of a repetition of an event that is associated with the primary afflictive emotions of grief or anger or the sensation of pain. Anger is the emotion we experience when something we expect is denied to us, and sorrow is what we experience when something that is ours is lost.

Li Chen: Why do you call these emotions primary, *sifu*?

Fu Hsiang: I call them primary, for the same reasons that artists refer to the three colours of red, green and blue as primary. We know that by suitably mixing these together, we can arrive at any shade we desire. Similarly every afflictive emotion is a compound of one or more of these three primary afflictive emotions.

Zhi Peng: Can you give an example?

Fu Hsiang: Well, let us take jealousy. We are doing a job, and one of our colleagues is very popular. Perhaps he is better than us, and so we feel the emotion of jealousy. But what is that emotion? First there is anger, because he has a talent that we would like to possess, but cannot. Second there is fear, because perhaps he will push us out of our own job. So jealousy is a compound of fear and anger provoked by the sight of some other person with something that we desire to have, but cannot possess.

Zhi Peng: Can you give me an example of a secondary afflictive emotion involving grief?

Fu Hsiang: Regret is a good example. Regret is accompanied by a sense of loss. We lost something through our own action, and we wish we could have it back. So regret is grief filtered through the memory of a past action that caused us to lose something we cherished.

Zhi Peng: Your theory is very interesting, *sifu*, but in Chinese medicine there are said to be more than three afflictive emotions. For example, worry is held distinct from fear. Are you saying that Chinese medicine is wrong?

Fu Hsiang: Chinese medicine is not wrong, Zhi Peng. You must remember that Chinese medicine classifies the emotions based on their effects on the organs of the body. The classification that they use reflects their medical understanding. In just the same way, an artist will classify colours according to the use to which he puts them, there is sky blue, and navy blue and many other blues. For him just to say 'this is blue' is not enough. But from the scientific view, there are only three primary colours of varying degrees of contrast.

You gave the example of worry. Worry is not an emotion distinct from fear. Worry is only a low level of fear held for a long period of time. Fright is an intense level of fear held for a very short period of time. They are separate in degree rather than kind. But Chinese doctors discriminate between the two, because the negative effects of these two emotions rebound on to different organs. Worry affects the spleen and fright the kidneys. Zhi, you studied chemistry?

Zhi Peng: I did some at college.

Fu Hsiang: Well then, you know that there are many poisonous chemicals. Now let us take as an example, the effects of mercury poisoning. In small quantities it causes gingivitis, mood swings and damage to the nerves. But in lethal doses it causes nausea, vomiting, diarrhea, and death by kidney failure. Though the very same substance is involved in each case, the medical effects vary according to dosage.

When we look at mercury as chemists, studying it for itself; then we make no discrimination between small and large amounts of mercury. Mercury is mercury. But as doctors we do discriminate, because the symptoms of poisoning are different.

Similarly as philosophers, when we study the afflictive emotions, we find that there are only three afflictive emotions. But if as doctors or psychiatrists, if we endeavour to treat people for their maladies, then we will make more discriminations in order to treat them more accurately.

Zhi Peng: I understand. But *sifu*, if this is the explanation of how people become corrupted, does this not show that the corruption is inherent in them and hence that they are not essentially good?

Fu Hsiang: This depends what you mean by essentially good. To say that a being has a property essentially, means for us that the being cannot lose this property without sustaining injury. People are essentially good because the afflictive emotions harm their body and soul. But if something is an essential property, meaning it is natural to them to enjoy this property, it does not follow that it is normal for them to have this property. People are naturally good, but they are not normally good. This arises from the fact that people are free to be perverse. The rest of the animal kingdom is bound by its essential nature, so that what is normal and what is natural coincide. Horses are both normally and naturally vegetarian.

Zhi Peng: But is the will to power not part of our essential nature, and does this not lead to the formation of afflictive emotions?   If so, it must be essentially evil.

Fu Hsiang: Tell me, is charcoal explosive?

Zhi Peng: No, *sifu*, it is not.

Fu Hsiang: And is saltpetre and sulphur explosive?

Zhi Peng: Neither of these things are explosive.

Fu Hsiang: Yet if they are mixed together in the right proportion, they make gunpowder, which is highly explosive.

Zhi Peng: That is true.

Fu Hsiang: The will to power is not evil in itself, any more than charcoal is explosive by itself.   It is the combination of the will to power with the basic facts of our incarnation into a material world which create the afflictive emotions.   The spirit itself is pure gold. But without this will to power, there is no possibility for our survival and evil is the price of its incarnation.

Zhi Peng: I see your point.

Fu Hsiang: Once the balance of the soul is disturbed by the afflictive emotions, excesses in action appear. The soul is then bound in a web of its own karma, and vulnerable to all the influences of which you and Li spoke in our last meeting. It is time to tend to other business. Zhi; you may demonstrate the cat stance.

The Ninth Discourse

On the Virtues

Li Chen: I have just met with Bo Tse, the famous Hsing-1[34] teacher. He was praising the merits of Hsing-1. His approach is to bear down fearlessly on the opponent and never to retreat, unless to renew his advance immediately. His students are taught Iron Shirt[35] and are trained to regard courage as the highest virtue.

Fu Hsiang: This is the manner of Mind and Form[36] boxing. The students are taught to be tough and resolute in action. Always meeting force with superior force. The fighting style is direct in its action, using tunneling and crushing power. The forearms of the Hsing-1 fighter are conditioned by *qi kung* to sweep aside all defence by their weight. It is not surprising that Bo Tse praises courage as the highest virtue, although there must be some question on this matter.

Li Chen: What is the master's opinion?

Fu Hsiang: As you know, my path is more contemplative than martial, even though I teach the martial art of *bagua* as a means of balancing the body. Like all things, I judge the value of something by its effect on the character and health of the person and courage is no different.

Li Chen: Could you explain this a little?

Fu Hsiang: If someone were to give me a herb, and I wished to know its effects. I would prepare a tincture[37] and administer the smallest amount to myself. I would observe the effects, and gradually increase the dosage until I could appreciate what it did.   Virtues like courage are no different. If we wish to understand them, then we must administer them in imagination and observe the effects on the character when they are administered.

Li Chen: This seems an interesting approach; would the master care to illustrate?

Fu Hsiang: In just the same way that we test a medicine, by beginning with a body free of medicine, so we must test the effects of the virtues by beginning with a character devoid of virtue.

Li Chen: This seems fair.

Fu Hsiang: Well, to begin, let's make an inventory of some evil qualities. Jealousy, hostility, rage, apathy, cowardice, fear, malice, dishonesty, selfishness, cruelty, bigotry, hypocrisy, greed, gullibility, paranoia, incoherence, indecision, lechery, gluttony, ignorance, slovenliness, self-hatred, misogyny — are not all these evil?

Li Chen: It is impossible to deny that they are evil.

Fu Hsiang: Let us name some of their contraries: friendliness, calmness, dynamism, courage, benevolence, honesty, altruism, kindness, liberality, sincerity, generosity, discernment, trust, eloquence, decisiveness, free-spiritedness, culture, wisdom, orderliness, and tolerance.

Li Chen: These are indeed virtues.

Fu Hsiang: It would be very unusual to meet anybody with all the qualities from one of these two lists. If we were to meet an individual, who manifested all the qualities from the first list and another, who manifested all those from the second list, who would we be drawn to?

Li Chen: The man who manifested all the vices in the first list, would be shunned by all those who knew him. But the good man would be loved by nearly everybody.

Fu Hsiang: Quite so. But could a man live for long when he is shunned by his fellow human beings, wracked with paranoia and unable to look after himself?

Li Chen: No, his life would be short and miserable.

Fu Hsiang: So our man of perfect evil is inherently unstable, like one of the physicist's transition elements that are brought to birth in an atomic furnace, only to decompose almost immediately into something else. He is not a sustainable entity in any sense. So here we see a property of evil that we touched on before.

Li Chen: What is that?

Fu Hsiang: Evil naturally tends to chaos. Whether it is a fire burning on a carpet where it does not belong, or a tumour intruding flesh where flesh is not wanted, it brings to termination the environment which is necessary to support it.   Do you think real evil men are totally evil in the way that our completely evil man is evil?

Li Chen: Our man of complete evil would seem to be a fiction. I have never known anybody or read of anybody whose character was as you described.

Fu Hsiang: Suppose we start with our completely evil man and begin our experiment by adding the medicine of virtue. Let's remove his cowardice and make him *daring* instead. Have we an improvement?

Li Chen: Well, if he is at least daring, then surely we have an improvement.

Fu Hsiang: Well, perhaps not. Our old version was a coward, so if he did hate you, it's likely that his cowardice would hold him back from doing anything about it. But the new version is daring enough to act on his hate as it impels him.

Li Chen: That is true.

Fu Hsiang: Of course, we still have indecision, but if we get rid of that, then there's little to hold him back. Do we not now have a psychopath?

Li Chen: This is a much more dangerous individual, certainly.

Fu Hsiang: Still he is only dangerous in a local sense; he is driven by selfish wants and desires. So let's take away his selfishness and make him *altruistic*. But he is now a degree more dangerous. He has graduated from the status of the local psychopath to a psychopath with a mission. Our new man will go out of his way to commit evil, convincing himself that it serves a higher purpose. He could very well go on to be a terrorist.

Li Chen: This is no improvement either.

Fu Hsiang: But if he's careless won't he make mistakes and get caught?

Li Chen: Quite probably.

Fu Hsiang: But suppose he is *orderly* and he's more dangerous again. He could kill hundreds before he's caught. Let's make him *calm* too, then he can keep his calm under questioning. Even when surrounded by police, he can lie his way out of it; keeping his explosive nature under check.

Li Chen: *Sifu*, the virtues you are adding are not improving him at all!

Fu Hsiang: It seems not. On the contrary, he simply gets more dangerous with each incarnation. But the list of evil characteristics left in him makes him a social outcast. So let us add a few good social characteristics; let us make him *charming*, so that he does not repel others. Let's make him *eloquent*, so that in addition to being able to mix with others, he can influence them.

Li Chen: This might do the trick.

Fu Hsiang: Now we have the makings of a leader, but without any conscience. He could rise to be a gang leader like Du Yuesheng.[38]

Li Chen: He was no model of virtue.

Fu Hsiang: Certainly not So let us add some tincture of the other good qualities. Let us add *culture*, so that he can act and dress properly in the best circles. Let us add not wisdom, but rather, the substitute that evil finds consistent with its purposes, *intelligence*. Let's make him *discerning*, so that he can see into the character of others. We now have a more lethal figure; a man with many of the qualities of a Hitler, a Pol Pot, a Torquemada, or a Stalin; with the power of personality to enslave others.

Li Chen: *Sifu*, we have tried to redeem our man of complete evil and turn him into a virtuous man, but we have so far succeeded only in producing a monster.

Fu Hsiang: When we progress deep in our mastery of the Tao, and learn to harness the elemental natures of our beings, we can acquire great power, including the power to influence others. If we do not learn to acquire real virtue, then we will fall prey to the dark side and become a servant of evil. But if such qualities as daring and altruism do not make a virtuous man, what do we have to add? What quality of character has to be added to make the transition from evil into good?

Li Chen: It seems, *sifu*, that what is missing is love and kindness.

Fu Hsiang: You are exactly right. All the great sages have recognised that love is the highest virtue, and indeed, the only essential virtue. All the others make us men of character, they add to our effectiveness as actors on this earthly stage. But what determines our essential nature with respect of good and evil is love.

Li Chen: This would seem to be true.

Fu Hsiang: We have discussed the virtues. A good example is the virtue of *generosity.* We all admire generous people, who are giving of their time and money for others. If you gave, say 100 *yuan* to a hungry person on the street, would this be generous?

Li Chen: 100 *yuan* is a lot of money; of course it would be generous.

Fu Hsiang: If Mr. Bill Gates were to do the same, would we regard this as particularly generous?

Li Chen: Probably not as generous as if you or I gave the money.

Fu Hsiang: Why not? The money is the same.

Li Chen: Because Bill Gates has so much money – 100 *yuan* is to him far less than one *yuan* to us.

Fu Hsiang: Suppose he was to give a million *yuan*, so he could have his photograph taken? Would this be generous?

Li Chen: No, this would be showing off.

Fu Hsiang: So it is not just a question of quantity, but the motive must be right?

Li Chen: That's right.

Fu Hsiang: If he were to give a million *yuan* to a hospital, with only the intent to serve others, would this be generous?

Li Chen: Yes.

Fu Hsiang: So we see that generosity, properly understood, is love acting through the medium of wealth, do you not agree?

Li Chen: I have never thought of it that way, *sifu*, but I suppose you are right.

Fu Hsiang: Now consider courage. Suppose two men hold up a bank, and shoot their way out against the odds, do we say they are courageous?

Li Chen: I don't think we would use that word.

Fu Hsiang: It would be certainly strange to read this title in a newspaper: "Courageous robbers kill five police in bank heist".

Li Chen: I think readers would protest.

Fu Hsiang: But if a man were to risk his life in saving another from drowning, we would call that courage.

Li Chen: Undoubtedly.

Fu Hsiang: So courage is really love acting through the medium of danger. Whereas to place oneself in danger for selfish ends is not courage, but simply daring.

Li Chen: That seems fair.

Fu Hsiang: Do you not know that kind of person, who possesses insight into others and can see their weaknesses, and uses that power to wound and manipulate?

Li Chen: Certainly, these people can cause great damage.

Fu Hsiang: But if we have this same ability, but use it in the service of love, then is this not wisdom?

Li Chen: It is.

Fu Hsiang: And if we are in a position of power over others, but lack any concern for their welfare, do we not tend to tyranny and injustice by seeking only our own advantage?

Li Chen: We do.

Fu Hsiang: But if on the contrary, we act from love for our fellow human beings, then we will be just and temperate?

Li Chen: That's right.

Fu Hsiang: So justice is love acting through the medium of power. Do you agree?

Li Chen: I do.

Fu Hsiang: Therefore whenever we see virtue at work in this physical world, we see the action of love manifesting through the appropriate faculty. Though each of us manifests different virtues, depending on his capacities and station, the essential nature of love remains the same.

The Tenth Discourse

On Love and the Soul

Zhi Peng: *Sifu*, tell me more about love.

Fu Hsiang: A man who has had so many girlfriends should not need instruction on the subject of love. This is an art for which you are famous. Why, not last week, I met you with your latest conquest.

Zhi Peng: Nonetheless, I would like to learn more about it, for you ended our last discourse by saying that love was the highest virtue.

Fu Hsiang: Well, you understand love; did you not say that you love chicken fried in coconut?

Zhi Peng: *Sifu*, you are making light of my serious intent.

Fu Hsiang: If I do, it is only to make a point. For people use the word lightly to mean whatever they particularly desire.

Zhi Peng: But how do you see it?

Fu Hsiang: Love is surrender. It is surrender of the self, of the ego, of the I. When one loves, one dies. There is an aphorism of an Indian master.

> Whoever seeks me finds me.
> Whoever finds me knows me.
> Whoever knows me loves me.
> Whoever I love I kill.

There is a killing in love. The killing is of the self. Therefore love is a return to the undifferentiated consciousness from which we came and to which we return. It is a brilliant fragment of a larger light.

When we truly love, the issues of self do not arise. The gap between the self and the beloved disappears. Therefore *self*-ishness is impossible. If the beloved is cold; we shelter her. If she is hungry, we feed her. If she is lonely, we caress her until her pain is gone. The great acts of sacrifice are inspired by love. Children are brought into the world through the sacrifice of the mother who through love bears that pain that allows them to live.

Being in love we experience the disappearance of the boundaries between ourselves and that which we love. But being in love can be a transient phenomenon. The human idea of love is often very different from what I have just described.

Zhi Peng: In what way?

Fu Hsiang: Human love is very often founded on the idea of self. We are unhappy and we want someone to put it right. We carry an image of the ideal person, man or woman.

In fact we are carrying a script, as for an actor. It contains the lines we want to hear. We then find a man or woman who seems right and we give them the script. "Please read this to me" we say "and be the person I want". Maybe the person does this. But already we have made a prison for them. When we first meet them, and we believe that we have found the right person for our script, we may feel great happiness, and may be "in love".

If our judgment is not too bad, and the person is happy with the lines, then things may go smoothly. But if our judgment is bad, then we have a case of infatuation.   The person is not the right person for the script, and we have fallen for an illusion.   This is a difference between infatuation and love. Love is based on knowledge; it has a clear sight. Love sees clearly because it is not tainted with the personal desires of the self. It does not deceive itself.

Even if our judgment is not too bad, our love is really conditional on the person giving us what we want. This will not go on forever. At some time the person will throw away the script. Then what do we do? Maybe get a divorce or like you, get another girlfriend. Or maybe we accept that the other person has their own needs too. This is acceptance. This is the beginning of true love and the foundation of compassion and mercy.

Zhi Peng: What you describe as love is hard to find.

Fu Hsiang: In this earthly realm it is, for the soul surrenders this quality in acquiring the will to power. For many people, what they call love is not love at all, but the desire to possess. True love is an invitation to return to the mode of consciousness that we enjoy between lives.

Zhi Peng: You mean the soul?

Fu Hsiang: Let us call it the spirit; that part of our being which is separate from the physical world and the afflictive emotions. The spirit exists in its own realm in a state of unity with the Tao. What we call the feeling of love is a reflection of that experience of unity at the level of personality. Consequently when we choose to experience the level of consciousness belonging to the spirit we experience it as a great influx of love. Because the experience of contact with the spirit is profoundly moving, we are tempted to ascribe moral qualities to the spirit and to go on to say that the spirit is also good. Now this is in a sense, partly right and partly wrong.

Zhi Peng: In what way?

Fu Hsiang: Both good and evil are qualities that link to the social world. They make sense only when we are surrounded by other sentient creatures distinct from ourselves. If I imagine myself into a universe where I am the only sentient being then my opportunities for good and evil are fairly restricted. I cannot swindle another person nor can I display generosity to him.

Since all conscious life is focused within me, the usual social obligations of proper conduct have no meaning.

In order to arrive at a state where good and evil are allowed to exist, a state of separation between me and others must have come into being. This is the proper meaning of the Fall. The fruit of the Forbidden Tree is the awareness of separation and the formation of the ego self. From this separation arises the possibility of treachery, deceit, lies on one hand and acts of altruism, and the overcoming of self-interest on the other.

This vast drama of greed, courage, betrayal and compassion are acted out at another level of consciousness. At the level of the ego self, it is natural to serve one's own self-interest. But from the level of the spirit, there is no separation between self and other and so when the consciousness of the spirit intrudes on the physical realm of human separation it brings with it that quality of selflessness that leads us to think of the spirit as good. In fact the spirit in itself is neither good nor evil; it transcends these qualities. It becomes good only in its interaction with our sense of separation where it impels us to act selflessly and from love.

Zhi Peng: What is the distinction between the spirit and the soul?

Fu Hsiang: When we are incarnated, the spirit infuses the body through a series of subtle sheaths, the densest of which is the physical body. This intersection of body and spirit is the soul. For this reason, as Taoists, we seek to nourish and balance the body, because there is no real distinction to be drawn between the two as long as we are alive. Any imbalance in the body will affect the soul.

Li Chen: But why did the spirit choose to become involved in the cycle of incarnation? Why abandon the higher realms for this hard existence?

Fu Hsiang: This is the most difficult question that you have asked. The unfolding of the Tao in matter and our own ensoulment within bodily form are surely part of the same process. Would you not agree?

Li Chen: It would seem that they are.

Fu Hsiang: So that a good answer to your question should answer the question "Why did the Tao issue in the world of form?"

Li Chen: This is also a good question.

Fu Hsiang: But not an easy one. Could we claim certainty on the basis of what our limited intellects can understand?

Li Chen: Possibly not, nevertheless, I would like to hear what the master has to say.

Fu Hsiang: What about this answer? One *qi kung* master of the Buddhist School, Li Hong-Zi[39], says that through past sins we fell into a point where destruction of the soul was a real possibility. However instead of being destroyed, the merciful powers of the universe placed us on the Wheel of Samsara[40], thereby guaranteeing us a chance to redeem ourselves.

Zhi Peng: But did we not reject this view in our earlier discussions?

Fu Hsiang: We did. It does not explain why the Tao should wish to issue a World of Form. If we are to understand why the transcendent Tao should issue in the World of Ten Thousand Things[41], we might understand the reason why our individual Spirits, which are reflections of the Tao, should become incarnated in bodies as well.

Li Chen: So what does the master think?

Fu Hsiang: The principle characteristic of matter is *limitation*. Limitation imposes constraints on our power and produces the conditions under which good and evil strive. It produces self-consciousness and a sense of separateness. But without limitation, none of the traditional virtues would have any existence.

Li Chen: Could you explain?

Fu Hsiang: Well, for instance, in a world where there is no danger and where wealth is unlimited and available to all, is there any sense to somebody being generous or brave?

Li Chen: It is hard to see how anybody could be brave in such a world. But we can be generous in other ways - with our time and our labour for instance.

Fu Hsiang: We have limited time available to us, so that when, without reward, I place my time at another's disposal I commit an act of generosity. But now suppose I have an infinite amount of time to use because I am immortal. Suppose that I can do an infinite number of things in a second of time. In such a case, does the idea of being generous with time and effort make sense anymore?

Li Chen: No. You are right; without limits there is no virtue.

Fu Hsiang: But since virtue is only a channel for love, if I cannot display virtue, how can I display love?

Li Chen: You cannot.

Fu Hsiang: Moreover, as we said, without limits there is no self-consciousness and no other to love.

Li Chen: That is true.

Fu Hsiang: So it is impossible for any being to experience love or to acquire these virtues without an environment that imposes limits; and this, spiritually, is the real purpose of our incarnation into matter.

Since love is the empowering virtue, the highest soul aspiration which we share is to give love to others.

The other virtues are simply expressions of love. But love for its action requires, limitation and separation and above all self-consciousness which requires that omnipotence has to be laid aside.

Li Chen: *Sifu* you are saying that the purpose of the unfolding of the Tao is to experience love?

Fu Hsiang: I am. For without the limitation of form, there is no good, there is no evil and there is no consciousness and there is no love. The purpose of the unfolding is for the Tao to experience love through becoming conscious of itself. Since we are expressions of the Tao, we are also the vehicle of its action, and so the highest aspiration of the soul is to overcome our separation through selfless love.

Notes

¹ In Chinese martial arts, disciples were divided into inner and outer door. Outer door disciples were taught the foundations of the practice, but were not taught the more advanced techniques. Inner door disciples were invited into the master's home. From one or two of the best inner door disciples, the next lineage holders were chosen who would succeed the master.

² Pa kua is an ancient Chinese martial art derived from a Taoist walking meditation.

³ Tai chi is another Chinese martial art. It can be practiced with a tai chi sword, which is a straight sword about 1½ inches wide and three feet long from end to end.

⁴ Part of the teaching of Buddhism. It advocates right understanding, right thoughts, right speech, right action, right livelihood, right effort, right mindfulness and right concentration.

⁵ The teaching or practice of Buddhism.

⁶ Fu Hsiang is expounding the principle of *substitutivity salva veritate*, which states that a denoting expression D which occurs in a sentence S and which denotes an

object E, can be replaced by any expression D' which denotes E without changing the truth or falsity of S. This principle is not universally true. An example from Bertrand Russell is "George IV wanted to know whether Scott was the author of *Waverley*". Though Scott is the author of *Waverley*, it is not true that George IV wanted to know whether Scott was Scott. In his argument, Fu Hsiang is using the applicability of this principle as a criterion for sentences that attribute properties to objects.

[7] A Chinese expression, literally translated as 'teacher-father'.

[8] Wu tai chi. One of the five classical forms of tai chi.

[9] Li Chen is referring to the Chinese annexation of Tibet in 1950.

[10] A unit of Chinese measurement; 2 *li* is one kilometer.

[11] In 1937, the Japanese came and ransacked Nanjing.

[12] The opening words of the *Tao Te Ching*, Lao Tse's famous book and one of the most sacred texts of Taoism.

[13] An ancient Chinese book dating from 800-1000 BC. Commonly used in China for divination.

[14] The black and white symbol representing the interplay of masculine and feminine; shown as a circle bisected by a wavy line with one side white and the other black and two spots of the opposite colour in each side.

[15] One of the traditional sites of Taoism in China. The Maoshan Taoists studied sorcery and magical techniques to gain power.

[16] Pa kua is a series of movements which are executed while walking in a circle. Students begin with a large circle and gravitate to a smaller one.

[17] A school of ethical thought called *emotivism*, which considers that ethical statements are only expressions of emotion and are devoid of sense. Sometimes called the 'boo-hurrah' theory of ethics.

[18] A school of ethical thought called *subjectivism* which holds that ethical statements are only reports about likes and dislikes.

[19] A school of ethical thought called *imperativism* which holds that ethical statements are like commands.

[20] A Chinese word meaning *energy* or *vital principle*.

[21] A Chinese unit of measure; slightly more than one yard.

[22] A Chinese unit of measure; 2 *jin* is one kilogram.

[23] A policy introduced in the 1980s in China, limiting couples to one child.

[24] Fu Hsiang's trifold distinction is found in the *I Ching* which uses the phrases 'inferior man', 'superior man' and 'sage'. Here he is plainly making some distance between Taoism and Confucianism. His highest model of virtue, the sage, is Taoist and follows the pattern described by Lao-Tse in the *Tao Te Ching*. His superior man is Confucian. There are some interesting parallels between Fu Hsiang's categorisation and Plato's distinction between men of brass, men of silver and men of gold, which he makes in the *Republic*.

[25] A position held by Kant, who argued that the person who did good out of principle rather than character, was to be preferred to one who did good out of character.

[26] A Confucian who lived 313-238 BC and who argued men were essentially evil and required the restraint of law.

[27] Another name for the study of the passage of *qi* through the body, and its effects on the organs of the body and the mind, which is the focus of acupuncture and other studies.

[28] The *yin* organs play an important part in the production and storage of *qi*.

[29] Zhi Peng is quoting Chinese medicine. Accounts vary on the identity of the afflictive emotions, some authorities recognise seven afflictive emotions.

[30] Yueh Fei was a twelfth century Chinese general who advocated armed resistance to the invasion of the Jin tribe. He was executed by the prime minister Qin Guei who desired peace.

[31] A phrase used in Taoism to refer to the trained body, which is soft and supple without, but tough and resistant within.

[32] A point about three inches below the navel.

[33] Fu Hsiang may be referring to the British empiricists who held that the mind was a *tabula rasa* or blank sheet, written on by experience.

[34] One of the three internal martial arts; *Hsing-I* fuses *qi kung* training with a direct attacking style.

[35] A form of *qi kung* whereby the body is made resistant to blows.

[36] Another name for *Hsing-I.*

[37] A preparation made by dissolving the herb in alcohol.

[38] A powerful gang leader, similar to Al Capone, who ruled the Shanghai underworld during the 1930s.

[39] Leader of the Buddhist sect of Falun Gong.

[40] The cycle of reincarnation.

[41] In Taoist creationism, the Tao existed in a state of stasis beyond duality. It split into *yin* and *yang* and, through a series of transformations, finally generated the World of Ten Thousand Things; i.e. the material universe.

WS - #0047 - 260422 - C0 - 197/132/10 - PB - 9781784562335 - Gloss Lamination